FAIROZ

Moniza Alvi was born in Pakistan and grew up in Hertfordshire. After working for many years as a secondary school teacher in London, she is now a freelance writer and tutor, and lives in Norfolk. Her latest books – all from Bloodaxe – are: *Fairoz* (2022); *Blackbird, Bye Bye* (2018); her book-length poem, *At the Time of Partition* (2013); *Homesick for the Earth*, her versions of the French poet Jules Supervielle (2011); *Europa* (2008); and *Split World: Poems 1990-2005* (2008), which includes poems from her five previous collections, *The Country at My Shoulder* (1993), *A Bowl of Warm Air* (1996), *Carrying My Wife* (2000), *Souls* (2002) and *How the Stone Found Its Voice* (2005). *The Country at My Shoulder* was shortlisted for the T.S. Eliot and Whitbread poetry prizes, and *Carrying My Wife* was a Poetry Book Society Recommendation. *Europa* and *At the Time of Partition* were selected as Poetry Book Society Choices in 2008 and 2013 respectively and both were shortlisted for the T.S. Eliot Prize. Moniza Alvi received a Cholmondeley Award in 2002. A collection of her poems was published in Italy by Donzelli Editore in their Poesia series in 2014, *Un mondo diviso*, translated by Paola Splendore. *Al tempo della Partizione*, also translated by Paola Splendore (an Italian version of *At the Time of Partition*), followed from Fuorilinea in 2020.

MONIZA ALVI

Fairoz

BLOODAXE BOOKS

Copyright © Moniza Alvi 2022

ISBN: 978 1 78037 600 4

First published 2022 by
Bloodaxe Books Ltd,
Eastburn,
South Park,
Hexham,
Northumberland NE46 1BS.

www.bloodaxebooks.com
For further information about Bloodaxe titles
please visit our website and join our mailing list
or write to the above address for a catalogue

Supported using public funding by
ARTS COUNCIL
ENGLAND

Cover design: Neil Astley & Pamela Robertson-Pearce.

Printed in Great Britain by Bell & Bain Limited, Glasgow, Scotland, on
acid-free paper sourced from mills with FSC chain of custody certification.

CONTENTS

How far can I follow her
my imagined Fairoz…?

Driving the devil away

He had to be stoned repeatedly.
The problem was the devil wouldn't die.

He had such a battering but he
rose up again, a living thing.

It was cathartic to hurl a stone at a wall
to combat the devil within –

the devil was no respecter of boundaries,
he permeated the skin.

It brought you closer to God,
helped to cast out unworthy desires.

'I want to feel the weight of a heavy stone,
to really be doing something,' said a boy.

'Take a small stone,' said his father.
'A pebble is enough.'

In the present tense

Fairoz wanders the dark pathways of the internet.
The trees form tunnels over her head.

People jump out of the bushes
each with something to say.

They pounce.
It's airless.

It's a way of leaving home.
Slurred voices in the night.

No moon. The planetary light of the screen.
Midnight. She sets off down the paths

without so much as a basket.
'It doesn't take long to meet a man,' they say.

A wayfarer.
He emerges from the trees

with an axe which he raises above his head.
She can see that he's smiling.

This kind of relationship
develops quickly.

Fairoz is very young. And not so young.
It's nice to have someone to talk to –

she thinks, she feels.
'I like your name,' he says.

Her name explodes in her head.
His name is Tahir.

She says 'I want to find out
why people do what they do.'

Indoors

It was cold. It was raw.
Their mother was a version
of the Snow Queen.

She could be so loving
to Fairoz and Annat
praising their rivering hair

and their progress at school
and saying how well blessed she was
to have such daughters.

At other times she hissed
and spat at them, their mother
who had herself been a little daughter.

How dried up she looked
when she looked in the mirror!
She smiled her best smile

and the room behind her
filled with snow
which soon became hard-packed.

Snow on the chairs and carpet
snow settling on the prayer mat
snow on the homework.

The hand-held mirror
grew so heavy.
When she dropped it

it flew into a thousand pieces
some of them no bigger
than grains of sand.

'Annat!' she called 'Fairoz!'
And they staggered towards her
across the indoor snow,

little pieces of mirror
shooting into them.
Half-blinded by flakes

the girls fell out into the garden.
No snow there, but greyness
and grit and the traffic

thundering on the ring road.
'We're getting too old to play.
And we're too cold.'

Slowly they went back indoors.
They observed their mother from afar
as if she were a distant relative.

Hair

Uncut
since birth
hidden or
on show
rippling loose
or shorn
falling across
a murderer's brow
hair is always
innocent.

What do you do with a heap of stones?

The stones would be so useful
for building houses.
So many houses are made of straw.
With only a little huffing
and puffing they're blown down.

'It was a house of female habitation'

Was it a house of mercy?
Three intelligent women lived there.
The two teenagers
looked around their in-between country.

They didn't know their father's name,
or they kept forgetting it.
He visited once – and left
at the same instant.

'Let me out,' he muttered.
He'd gusted in from the East,
had no money to speak of.
The door opened of its own accord.

෨ঌ

Questions in the wood

She logs on. The light of her screen.
Tahir stands, legs apart in the clearing.

'How old are you, Tahir?'

He laughs.
'I'm much older than you. Guess how old?'

'I think you're twenty-five, no thirty.'

He laughs again. 'Right the first time.'

'What do you do, Tahir? Do you work?'

'It's complicated. I'll tell you very soon...
You're so pretty,' he says.

She's there with him, out in the open.
He puts down his axe.
His eyes are quite gentle.

'Tahir, do you pray? Five times a day?
Does Allah listen?'

'That's a big question, Fairoz.
He does. Usually He does.'

The Devil and the gleams

Tahir's eyes gleam.
His axe gleams.

And on the screen's dark sky
a single star gleams.
Shrinks. And disappears.

A gleam is
something to work with.

The Devil's soup –

brought to boiling point each day at noon
and smelling of all things rotten.

'God, would you like to try some?'

God spits it out.

What was I doing tasting the Devil's soup?
Can any good come of it?

The white cat

'Amma, Amma, can we have a cat?
We'll look after it, we'll feed it.'

'We're too near the ring road,' Amma said.
She frowned – and the window frosted up.

A cat walked in, white as the indoor snow.
It lifted each paw high at the shock

of the cold and wet.
Within seconds its eyes froze shut.

Not enchantment

When her screen lights up she steps through it.
Signposts point in all directions –

some are broken.
Not this way. She's back where she started.

Internet wanderers step forward then melt
into the trees. She can't grasp

what they're saying.
She knows she's a wanderer too.

Where's Tahir?

'See you next time.' That's what he said.

'Tahir! Tahir!' She can't see anyone at all.

Just the angry red stalks of the brambles
and lots of clingy frilled mushrooms.

She shuts the screen down.
And for a few moments she's nowhere.

The night is half-blind.
Schoolclothes on a chair.

Her headscarf like moonlight
touching the floor.

In the morning

she says to herself:

'I don't like my life.' And again.
'I-don't-like-my-life.'

Lifecoldlife.

Sun creeping through the curtains.
Pale sun.

And now on the way to school
'I don't like my life because —— '

The Devil enjoys 'I don't like my life.'

He echoes the words:
'I don't like my life! I don't like my life!'

It's familiar to him – this chink.
This fast-widening crack.

Home

The first time she heard it
it took her a moment to take it in.

'Go home!' She was just by the house,
walking up the short front path.

She dropped her bag on the doorstep,
turned and picked up a stone.

But he'd already slid away.
He left his two poison words.

Fairoz and Annat

'Fuck off!' she said quietly. 'Fuck off!'

She knows *We don't swear.*
But now she swears a lot, under her breath.
And sometimes louder. Stonewords.

'Why do you swear so much, Fairoz?'

'Because I'm older. Because I want to.
And I need to. That's why.'

As summer

As summer belongs to the year.
And winter too.

And the house belongs to the road.
Or seems to.

As nakedness belongs to the light
as well as the dark.

As the surface belongs to the depth
whatever the depth is like.

As the tongue belongs to speech –
though not to all speech.

As our heads belong to our bodies.
And have to.

School lunchtimes

Ihdinas-siraatal mustaqeem
'Guide us to the straight path'

In the second-floor room
('somewhere for us –
Muslim girls')
after midday prayers
she thinks of Tahir
the things he says:
'I've a day off
next week –
shall we meet?
Fairoz, tell me
how long is
your hair?'

Listening to Fairoz and Tahir

To shut out other sounds,
to be the curved surface

their voices bounce against,
to put the unsaid on one side.

To eavesdrop on them,
to overhear and underhear,

and attend with my faulty ear
to a made-up conversation
                                attempting

with my own words
to hold my own words back.

TAHIR: What would you do for Allah?
He needs us, you know. They hate us here.

FAIROZ: Yeah, I know that. Most of them do –
they treat us like shit. We pray…

TAHIR: Praying is all very well. But we must
be braver that that. We owe it to Allah
as an act of faith. Fairoz, I'd like to meet,
really meet. Just for a short time.
Tomorrow? Today? In the park?

FAIROZ: Yeah. Later today? Really meet.

Pilgrims

'a great joy'
'my whole family is here'
    'it's something I've so much wanted to do'
'marvellous, if you can afford it'
   'I'd always dreamt of making the pilgrimage to Mecca'
'over two million annually'
       'almost like a vacation'
       'peaceful – no worries'
'carrying the flags of our countries'
        'I had the most incredibly good night's sleep'
   'when I was 15 years old my father sent me on the Hajj alone'
'we all learned to adapt and make the best of it'
       'a bit like a really massive sleepover'
     'posting photographs on Facebook'
'a combination of nerves and heightened euphoria'
    'simple Ihram clothing – all of us equal under the eyes of God'
     'measures are taken to prevent cholera'
   'the exploitation of pilgrims'
'there's a risk'
    'stoning the devil is the most dangerous part of Hajj'
'pilgrims have been asphyxiated, crushed to death'
     'like being caught in a wave'
  '110 degrees – people dying of thirst'
       'some without shoes'
'pilgrims throwing water bottles into the crowd'
      'I was walking like a dead man'
     'the push and pull of the crush stripped the clothing off people'
'a terrible day in Hajj history'
    'I became very sick during the time'
  'I injured my leg and needed stitches and still have a scar'
      'Hajj makes all things bearable'

'even death can be welcomed'
'once in my life, to be here'
'It was... sort of my duty to Allah'
'I'm very happy today'

Does the Devil know what he is?

Does he even have knowledge?
Does the Devil have instincts?

Ah, the Devil has only the diabolical.
He grips it tight.

The notice

> **THE MOSQUE IS
> OPENING ITS DOORS
> TO THE HOMELESS
> ANY RACE OR CREED.**

'Fairoz, shall we help? Will you?'

'I'll think about it, Annat.'

———————

What would you do for Allah?
What would you do?
What wouldn't you do?

For Allah.

        For Allah?

When they meet

Tahir fishes in a pocket.
Retrieves a small parcel
loosely wrapped.

'For you, Fairoz!'

She slides out a bangle, elfin, gold –
a gift for a fairy-child.

'Thank you. But it's tiny…'

'Let me try.'

He steadies her wrist, grasps
the shining circle, pressing it
until her hand is red.

'Sorry,' he says.

A story of God and the Devil

Someone or something
gave birth to them –
countless years ago.

They looked at each other
with recognition.
Occasionally they swapped roles.

God was fully capable of
ripping an arm open.

Sometimes the Devil
normally so active
floated downriver on a log.

Let me be God for the day.
Let me be the Devil.

Ripe

'Ha!' said Amma. 'Ha!
Choose your own?
And where will you find him –
under a stone?'

The time ran ripe
as a juicy peach
a nectarine or pear.
It was a beautiful alarming thing.

A shadow bent papery
by the door.
Who's that? Boy or girl?
Shall we ask the shadow in?

They wanted to choose.
It was summer in the house.
The time was ripe. More than ripe.
'They're our lives, Amma, not yours.'

Wolves-of-the-woods

Wolf-crouching-by-fragile-trees

wolf-bored-bored

wolf-where-the-streams-never-stop

wolf-with-grievances-going-back-generations

wolf-with-enquiring-eyes

wolf-drifting-like-smoke

wolf-and-a-small-patch-of-blue-sky

wolf-I'll-never-forget-what-they-did-never

wolf-where-the-dark-streams-converge

wolf-in-a-tiny-minority

wolf-a-more-attractive-husband-than-a-suitor-
   in-a-lost-to-the-world-village

wolf-where-the-streams-run-shallow

wolf-as-cruel-as-a-savagely-beaten-thing

wolf-long-thin-blade

wolf-howling-on-a-high-note

wolf-with-an-unread-Guide-to-the-Koran

wolf-with-a-grey-coat-and-military-buttons

wolf-reciting-half-a-prayer

wolf-where-the-wood-is-suddenly-a-forest

What runs under her skin

Can anyone know
what's inside her?

Can I?
    Hardly.

Do her thinking
and her doing collide?

Or are her outside
and inside aligned?

Who is she? Who can say?
Can she say?

            I can only

let her unfold.

TAHIR: I can show you Jannah. Can you picture
Heaven, Fairoz?

FAIROZ: Dunno.

She pictures Jannah

Gardens   higher than the sky   not where weeds grow   rivers
valleys of pearls and rubies   no cars no buses   all the gates
a bit like the park gates   taller with names   try to see it   angels
questioning   seeing angels   no sadness   joy for you   forever
if you've led a good life   only if   Allah deciding when people die
Judgement Day   Jannah   who will go there?   definitely go?
everlasting life   a glow   smiling not talking   forgiveness
Jannah   Paradise   not on this earth

Absent and present

He has to go away now.
Go away for a while.
To where?
Not there... nor there...
but still very far away.
Though nowhere is far away.
He assures her they'll
never be far away.
They can still spend hours
talking in the woods
tomorrow – and today.

TAHIR: Forgot to say. Something crucial about Jannah. Fairoz you know about those who die defending Islam, they go through the Baab Al-Jihad. That's their gate into Heaven. Know about that gate?

FAIROZ: Sure. Yeah. I know about that one.

TAHIR: Defend Islam. That's what we've got to do.

Her absences

The noughts
in the teacher's register.

O

Unauthorised.

O

Disappearing into a zero.
Gravely at risk.

O

Where is she? Where are they?
What is she learning?

O

Falling through the

O

Under the railway bridge
in the dankness

O

with a boy-man,
a man-boy. Or is she

O

alone in her bedroom
with the curtains drawn

O

and still meeting a man?

O

Fairoz! Fairoz!

O

Lost in the fog of the

O

the blank that aches
and enlarges.

O

'where the swarm is thickest'

Indoor snow again.
The house was full of it,
flake after flake
all the white bees swarming.

'Amma, it's freezing! Where are you?'

'I'm upstairs WORKING, Fairoz.
And don't be stupid, it's not at all cold.'

FAIROZ: The more you try to forget, the more you can't forget… Yeah, that's what I think.

TAHIR: Yeah. When I was a kid our town was
mostly white and our window was smashed
so many times there was no point mending it.
When they banged on the door we hid upstairs.
Like we couldn't exist. I can't forget that.

The dark patch

Once there was a young person who bought some cream
for lightening the skin. It wasn't for what you think.
It was just that she had a small darker patch on her chest
and she wanted to lighten it. She thought it was terrible
when those like her with brown skin, girl or boy, wanted
to lighten their whole skin, their face. This was only
a dark patch. She didn't want that. That was all.
But then she thought she might get a too-light patch
and it would stand out. Was a too-light patch as bad as
a too-dark patch? Was the cream worth risking?
The dark patch preyed on her mind. It wasn't on her face,
but still it was on her mind. Darker than it should be.
The small browner patch that she couldn't get away from.
Then the thought of a light patch nagged at her.
The skin-lightener in its white pot.

The plants

The Devil was scattering seeds.
God's curiosity was roused.
'What are you growing?'

'Plants, tough plants, God.
They take root in the unlikeliest places,
force their way up
through those tiny cracks.
I call them shrivel-the-soul.
One glimpse can be enough.'

God had at least to equal this.
'My perfect flowers...' he began.

It was long ago

And not so long ago

that Amma forced a piece of ice
into her hand, not a word spoken.

It stuck there like a burr. Ice with hooks.

'Amma! Amma!'
In the palm of her hand
a cold flame was burning.

A conversation

The child and the adult
she'll soon become
are walking hand in hand
through the bushes.
Sometimes the adult leads.
Sometimes the child.

'I'm ready now,' says the child.
'Ready for what?' asks the adult.
The child ignores the adult's question.

ANNAT: Salma's sister, you know, she takes her salwar kameez off and wears jeans just to put the bins out!

FAIROZ: What they make us do! The little things – I reckon they're big things.

ANNAT: Wish we could just get on with our lives...

A punch

Sorry sorry she said sorry   did she mean it?   Tahir said
sorry too   did he mean it?   sorry   it's just a word   felt
guilty   she'd asked for it he said that   punch   quick
like a boxer   nobody there to see it   she made him do it
sorry   maybe   probably she had   thinking thinking
did he think that?   hurts   arm throbs   she must have
he was usually kind   but now this   wear it   not for me
he said wear it for Allah   cover your face   now he's
saying sorry again   soft word sorry   it depends
how it's said   swelling   ow!   No!   like 'I love you'
depends how it's   ways to say things   words said

Ice age

It had been there forever.
and yet at the back of their bones

they knew there was something different
and that was the strange thing.

Cold spoke in its own tongue,
its words were a glacial stream.

Who could ever really escape an ice age,
protect themselves

from the indoor or outdoor cold?
Who could avoid all the stone

the ice-rivers carried
and the sediment left behind?

The cold bore ice and more ice –
thick sheets of it

to the hemispheres of the house.
It scratched and scoured

the human core.

He's 'v v sorry'

From Tahir   buds opening slowly   colours of flames

tulips! tulips swaying   dancing in a circle   faster

fasterfaster   sprawling out   out   dying   colour

of blood   and beginning again   closing   opening

closing in her phone   shut in it   tulips not real

luckily   only she'll see them   secret

The short long story

More than now and then
since tenuous time began

in what was contortedly
called the world of men

under the thwarted sun
under the guarded moon ——

'So, what kept happening?'

All that is tortuous
between East and West.

The loping wolf

I'm a wolf of strong faith
in a land of disbelief.

I know my strengths
and knew what to do –

I applied for the night-work.
I'm always on time.

With my razor-teeth
I'm a biter –

limbs, balls, breasts,
I fasten on hard, dig in.

If they're released
from my chamber

they leave with a solemn
hooded look.

I'll lope to the war
of everywhere, East-West

West-East. Only God
can lope this far.

A tale reduced to a sliver

Once, in the middle of the last century, a student crossed
to this country by boat. He wore his smartest clothes.
He had to look for somewhere to live. The signs didn't say
NO BLACKS then, but nevertheless it was difficult.
He was an outsider and he was poor. He found an old hut
at the edge of the town by the airfield. Padlocked. Long.
It looked spacious. He made enquiries.

'That hut by the airfield. Can I live there?' he asked.
'There's nowhere else.'

'Nobody can live there,' they said. 'It's not fit for
human habitation! It's a disused Nissen hut.
There'll be rats and mice.'

'Compared to where most people live where I
come from, it's a palace!'

'All right,' they said, in the end. 'But it might only be
for a while. We'll have to see.'

He moved in straight away, with another student
from home. The hut was certainly long – and large.
There was a stove with a pipe going up to the roof.
The rain pounded on the corrugated metal.
Every day they killed rats and mice.

FAIROZ: Some fights are good fights. Yeah.

TAHIR: Yeah. Against the West. WESTERN extremists.
They won't say they are. The hypocrites! The shits!
Someone I know, their uncle was imprisoned, tortured by
westerners for nothing. They thought he was someone else.
They never apologised.

FAIROZ: They just say it's us! And

TAHIR: Listen – we were great once, way back. And we'll
be great again. We're global already you know.

God's eyelids

For an hour or two God lay down
in the shade of a wide-canopied tree.

'Wake up!' laughed the Devil who
always had to keep track of him.
'You don't have time to sleep!'

'I'm not asleep,' said God. And sighed.
Each eyelid was as heavy as a war.

This woman will speak to you, he says

A woman
steps forward into the clearing.

She carries an axe.

Her voice smiles.
Her words rush and tumble:

> 'Fairoz   listen   we need intelligent girlslikeyou   clever and brave
> there's hardly anywhere safe   notyet   but we'll look after you
> don't be afraid   you'll be verywellrewarded   there're lots of us
> but specially picked   we're like sistersmothersbestfriends.'

She hasn't finished yet.

> 'Look I'll message you,' she says.

And disappears into the trees.

The bride

'Let's marry – online. I can arrange it.'

> She knows about it now.
> This marriage in the woods
> must be valid
> all in one sitting
> with a wali and witnesses
> gathered around.
> And with no interruptions
> not a nightbird's hoot.
> The couple sufficiently lit.

'I love you, Fairoz. Well, what do you think?'

> In the semi dark,
> off the twisting paths
> she sees
> a man is marrying
> a girl.
> How young is this bride?
> Hard to tell.
> Why is she looking down?

'For now and for the afterlife.'

> The girl's dress is so heavy
> and the wood is tangled.

Gone

Like a strip of land,
a swathe of forest, has she gone?
She hasn't gone abroad,
or travelled very far at all.
She quarrels with her sister,
eats dal and rice and sleeps, at home.
She says her prayers.
She takes the normal route to school
where she goes drifting – out.
The teachers say 'Is something wrong?
We're here if you want to talk to us.'
Her friends? She's let them slip away.
She's on her phone upstairs,
her schoolbag unopened on the floor.
She's edging out of one story,
looking both ways. Not looking.
She hasn't left – but she has gone.

A task

Can you sew?
asked the woman in the wood.
I believe you can.

Not a button, not a shirt,
a jacket or a dress –
can you sew a vest?

I know you're skilled enough
with Allah on your side
to do a good neat

lasting job.
It's not just women's work –
it's for our cause, you know.

I'll give you strong thread
to feed through the empty eye
of a silver needle.

Can you stitch life to death
and pull the thread tight?
A few sharp tugs, and that's it.
An honourable thing, this sewing.

FAIROZ: You can get to Heaven, then, if you've killed someone, yeah?

TAHIR: I've told you, there's killing – and there's killing. It depends... If you kill defending Islam, Allah will welcome you. Yeah. He'll open that special gate. Remember the Baab Al-Jihad. It's the main thing to remember that gate. It's the most crucial thing of all. It's not murder. It's faith. And it's honour. And... and Allah will witness it.

He always knows why you did it. You're clever, Fairoz – I know I can trust you not to forget.

The Viewing

She clicks 'Play'.
Two – lit up.
An axe-man.
A prisoner.
Shadowy others.
Tall trees spaced.
Axe swings to
neck.
She clicks 'Pause'.
A loneliness.
She clicks 'Play'.
Sees it.
Seen it.
Sees it.
Dark now.

He was

He was
a traitor.
You hear me, Fairoz?
OK?

The contest

God held one end of the argument
and the Devil, the other. They heaved
and strained but nothing ever

moved much. The two of them
locked in a tug-of-war.
The rope they couldn't drop.

A change

It was different now. Tahir was different.
He'd been different before
but now the difference was – different.
'You're different now, Tahir.'

'No, I'm not – I love you more
than I did before. That's all
that's different.
Every day is different!
Let's have no more talk
of different.'

Classroom scorpions

Out of the big smeary window   the city
and more and more of it   a grey sea
so quiet from up here   like empty

'Note what Macbeth says to Lady Macbeth.
Page 93. Act III, Scene 2… Line 36…
Found it, Fairoz?

'O, full of scorpions is my mind, dear wife!'

TAHIR: Fairoz – let's get married. Like I say. Be strong together. I keep picturing Paradise – and praying. You're my reward. Ha! So what do you reckon? About being my wife. A proper wife.

FAIROZ: A wife? A proper wife? Leaving home? And doing what married people do?

TAHIR: Of course. What else? Living together. Our home. I can picture it. Easily. Yeah, I'd really like that.

Cherry stones

Tinker

Tailor

Martyr

Sailor

Rich

Or poor

Or very poor

West

Or East

Or in between

Woman beater

Freedom fighter

Bomb maker

This life

Next life

Sometime

Never

Who's there?

That time   in the playground   blood-red voices
couldn't not hear them   'Murderer! Murderer!'
older ones   younger ones joining in   and one clear
piping voice 'You're all murderers!'   words thrown
ducked   threw back 'Murderers yourselves!'
couldn't deal with it   not really   not at all   words
gouging   we're all humans they're not   should she
tell?   Amma?   the teacher?   maybe   no
no point   what would they do?   could make things
worse   yeah   an unfairness   bigger than

And now   long after   and not so long after
looking at her hands   her shoes   and into
the chasm   behind her eyes   to see   to see
who's there   him   her   us   'Murderers!'
Murderers?   no   yes   no   who's there
in the seething?

DANGER

The explosives in their containers:

hydrogen peroxide, sulphuric acid,
ammonium nitrate, potassium perchlorate…
They carry triangular warning signs.

The emotions are also dangerous.
                              Even sadness

transmuted into something else.

TAHIR: Your sister – would she help us? Help the cause?
She's religious, isn't she? Is she... reliable?

FAIROZ: No... No. Don't think she'd help. She'd say
'You can give to charity if you want to help Allah.'
Or something like that. She's good...

TAHIR: So I'm not good? You're not good?

FAIROZ: We are... But not in the same way.

The eye

O hardware shop.
O faithful eye –

has it seen anything unusual?
The hardware shop is dark

and so densely forested.
How can the recording eye see?

But it does. It's well-trained.
The forester is quick and deliberate.

The hammers are ranged like
strong-beaked birds

on the bristling wall-rack.
A claw hammer, that's it.

And a club hammer.
Drops them into the open cage

of his basket. Adds long nails.
Hurries to the wooden counter.

Something not right? He's too
intent, no glancing around.

Someone wants to hammer a nail
through the universe.

Does the eye weep?
The eye is dispassionate.

She's heard nothing from Tahir

'Speak soon.' That's what he said.
'Speak soon love you Fairoz.'

And now she

    cuts herself on the ice of waiting
    cuts herself on the ice of not knowing
    cuts herself on the ice

Call him three times

Tahir? said the woman in the wood.
Who's Tahir? Oh you mean Abdul.
He's really Abdul. Sometimes
Anwar. Names are a risk.

I don't think you'll see him,
not for a while. Maybe
not in this life.
He was always careful,

so very skilled at
covering his tracks.
But it's hard
to hide in these woods.

Don't despair. Inshallah,
no one need be lonely here.
Friendship, marriage –
just footsteps away.

But try calling him now.
Three times, once for each name.
Abdul – Anwar – Tahir.
He'll answer, if he hasn't moved on.

What's real?

Did she know him?   Abdul? Anwar?   alive? or dead?
heard nothing from him   like death   maybe he can't
contact her? doesn't want to?   where is he? where?
nobody knows   or nobody will tell her   he could be
anywhere   the wide-open anywhere   hunted down
running running   hiding   forgotten her   by now
yeah talking to someone else   like being kicked ——
keep trying to find him?   pull away?   all the hours
talking   but then he lied   like kept big secrets from her
Jannah   what he said that he'd be there and she'd
be there   somehow they'd be together   not real
a million miles from real   pull away can't

The Devil's news

'What's the point of having good news
if I can't relay it directly to God?
My devastating, appalling good news.
I'll run through fire with this news.
Running to you, God. Running.
Swifter than the speed of your light.
Listen. Oh God. Such news.'

Witnesses

'he was keeping out of view'
'it seemed strange he was just standing there'
    'a feeling of being hurled to the side'
'then there was another bit of hell'
  'I saw things I'm never going to be able to unsee'
'I wanted to help'
    'we tried to outnumber him'
'I was aware of people moaning and calling out'
     'there was screaming, blood and chaos'
  'I saw his arm move quickly'
    'I kept talking to her, trying to keep her conscious'
'someone shouted Mind your backs!'
'I had to make sure someone wasn't being beaten to a pulp'
    'I rushed to the other side of the stairwell to get away'
'people were yelling Keep moving!'
    'armed police surrounded him'
'the officer shouted Don't move!'
  'we were trying desperately to apply first aid'
'a man was wrestling with a person lying on the ground'
   'the guy on the floor opened his jacket and we backed away fast'
  'he charges towards the guy'
    'he was clearly wearing something protective'
  'someone tried to stop me going to help'
'my leg was damaged, I kind of dragged it along'
    'I tried to comfort him'
  'I took a moment to Tweet'
   'I used my belt to apply a tourniquet'
  'I was completely overwhelmed'
   'I didn't think of leaving'
'it's got nothing to do with religion, nothing at all'
     'if it happened today, it could happen tomorrow'

In the snow

She lay down in the indoor snow –
it numbed her slowly, very slowly.

'You not going to school, Fairoz?'

'What's wrong with you then? Tell me.'

'Annat, do you know what's wrong with Fairoz?'

Her whole life

She hasn't   she didn't   luckily she hadn't   she did
just a bit   not really   more than a bit   no   a little
and she watched   will the police?   they'd want to
track her   doesn't want to lie doesn't   was drawn in
interested   drawn in drew out   drew in (don't say that)
doesn't want to lie   listening listening   did a lot of
listening to him   to her to all of them   was so tired
of all the listening   what did she really think?   it was
wrong   not completely no yes   violence like murder?
she has her life   she's young not so young   no
will they think she's young?   responsible like guilty?

Could someone help her?   she has this one life   hers
she's an intelligent girl yeah   more than quite intelligent
her whole life sometimes it's nothing   though not nothing

Urgent question

'Mirror mirror,
heart of silver, not of gold,
am I young – or am I old?'

'Come closer now...
The answer is
young-old. Old-young.'

Like a mark on her kameez

Spreading like a mark, a stain
very fast
out of her control.
Stigma.
       More strongly there
even than herself.

What she'd like to say

She always, almost
always (especially later)
had her doubts –

They crept in like waves

sometimes smaller
sometimes larger –

that he was good
that what he said
was good *was* good –

She never let him
put words into her mouth.

Is there anything she'd like to say?
'I had my doubts. Yeah, doubts.
I'm telling you the truth.'

The room in her mind's eye

One of the chairs
is for her.
Pulled out for her. No —
screwed to the floor.
A window? No window.
A metal grille.
Walls made of blocks.
An inside lock? Maybe not.
She can't sit down
on a chair wedged
into the corner
of her mind's eye.
It's a big enough room
for the corner of an eye.
Bolts? No clock?

The woods

The woods are the woods –
nothing more. The trees

darkening the pathways.
People still jump out of the bushes

but with nothing new to say,
their mouths opening and closing.

The woods – there's no beginning
and no end. The woodcutters

are at work. Strewn branches.
Tree-stumps are everywhere now,

as many stumps as trees.
And crowds of mushrooms.

Those that look so enticing are deadly –
the pristine white ones, white as

white feathers, cap and gills,
and the storybook red ones

with white spots – warty really.
They attract the flies – and kill them.

This place. Where is she?
Past tense. Where was she?

Cold song

Her teeth are chattering
chatter chatter
but she hasn't told
told no one
chatter chatter no one
reflects her words
back to her
can anyone bear to hear it
hear her wake up

Her future

'Another one for me,' said the Devil.
'I seize my chance, get a hold

and in the end
what can you do about it?'

God thought for a moment.
He didn't need to say anything.

But he did.
'We'll see who wins,' he said.

'Over every soul there is a watcher'

A star to watch over you
not just to watch you
a piercing star
if this could be true
if the beautiful ideas
could really be beautiful
and stay beautiful

a protecting star
a vigilance
a kindly watcher star
not just record-keeping
and the nights not starless
if this night-star could be true
in some sense true.

My imagined Fairoz

How far can I follow her
my imagined Fairoz – she has
no map and nor have I –
                    follow her

into her house of three women
one older, one younger
a breathing house

a house of stopped breath
where she lives and doesn't live,
follow her into her room –

follow her inside and out,
as far – further than I can?
How far can I follow her

and then – choosing the time
while not exactly choosing it –
let her go?

Notes and Acknowledgements

11: 'The stoning of the devil', *Rami al-Jamarat*, is one of the main rituals of the annual Hajj pilgrimage to Mecca. Small stones are thrown at three walls, symbolically driving the devil away. The ending of this poem drew inspiration from an article by Naser Al Wasmi in *The National*, 22 August 2018.

18: 'It was a house of female habitation': The title and first line are derived from Stevie Smith's poem 'A House of Mercy', *The Collected Poems and Drawings of Stevie Smith*, edited by Will May (Faber and Faber, 2015).

30: *Ihdinas-siraatal mustaqeem* 'Guide us to the straight path' is from the Muslim prayer: 'Surah Al-Fatihah'.

33: 'Pilgrims': Includes variants on comments in *Records of the Hajj: The Pilgrimage to Mecca* (Cambridge University Press, 1993), ed. D.L. Rush and 'Hajj Stories' from the British Museum's exhibition: 'Hajj: Journey to the heart of Islam' 26 January–15 April 2012.

49: 'where the swarm is thickest': The title and the image of the 'white bees' is taken from Hans Christian Andersen's *The Snow Queen*, translated by H.B. Paull (Hythloday Press, USA, 2013).

50: 'The more you try to forget' was partly inspired by an account of racist violence in Mark Townsend's book *No Return* (see Acknowledgements below).

61: 'The loping wolf' was partly inspired by an account of torture in Azadeh Moaveni's book *Guest House for Young Widows* (see Acknowledgements below).

67: 'wali' – 'authority figure' at a Muslim wedding, often the bride's father.

77: 'Cherry stones' is derived from a traditional fortune-telling counting game. The most common English version is 'Tinker, Tailor, Soldier, Sailor, Rich Man, Poor Man, Beggar Man, Thief.'

82: 'She's heard nothing from Tahir' was inspired by a line in the poem 'Difference' by Anna Kamieńska in *Astonishments: Selected Poems of Anna Kamieńska,* translated from the Polish by Grażyna Drabik and David Curzon (Paraclete Press, Massachusetts, 2018).

87: 'Witnesses': Includes variants on eye-witness responses in newspaper reports of incidents of extremist violence.

98: 'Over every soul there is a watcher' was initially inspired by lines from *The Koran* as in Arthur J. Arberry's translation from the Arabic (Oxford World's Classics, Oxford University Press, 2008), LXXXVI 'The Night Star': 'And what shall teach thee what is the night-star? / The piercing star! / Over every soul there is a watcher.'

*

I would like to thank the editors of the following publications in which selections from *Fairoz* have appeared: *Bad Lilies, Kitaab: The Best Asian Poetry 2021*, edited by Sudeep Sen, *Poetry London, Poetry Wales, Pratik* (Nepal), *The Poetry Review* and *Wasafiri*.

The poem 'Ripe', in an earlier version, was included in a group of poems I contributed to *Turning the Page: Celebrating 40 years of Southall Black Sisters*, edited by Rahila Gupta (Southall Black Sisters Press, 2019).

*

I'd like to pay particular tribute to the following books:

NON-FICTION:

Azadeh Moaveni: *Guest House for Young Widows: Among the Women of Isis* (Scribe Publications, London, 2019).

Mark Townsend: *No Return: The True Story of How Martyrs are Made* (Guardian/Faber, London, 2020).

NOVELS:

Karan Mahajan: *The Association of Small Bombs* (Vintage, London, 2017).

Kamila Shamsie: *Home Fire* (Bloomsbury, London, 2017).

Meike Ziervogel: *Kauthar* (Salt Publishing, Cromer, 2015).

DRAMA:

Nyla Levy: *Does My Bomb Look Big in This?* (Methuen Drama, London, 2019; on UK tour in 2019).

Gillian Slovo: *Another World: Losing Our Children to Islamic State* (Oberon Books, London, 2016).

*

Thank you to the Consortium for the Humanities and the Arts South-east England (CHASE) for the funding which supported the writing of *Fairoz*.

*

With gratitude to Denise Riley and also to Jeremy Noel-Tod at the University of East Anglia.

Thank you to Southall Black Sisters and editor Rahila Gupta for the commission, and to Harleen Dhillon, Sheena Mohammed, and Aline Thomas for their inspiring contributions to *Turning the Page*.

Thank you to the National Theatre poetry group and the Norwich group for their thoughtful feedback.

Many thanks to Susan Wicks, Heidi Williamson and Jackie Wills who read and commented on the manuscript, and thank you also to Jane Duran.

Thank you to Gary Williamson for valued help with research, and thank you also to my editor, Neil Astley, for his care and suggestions.

And my thanks to my husband Bob and to my daughter Alice.